Beauty of
Maryland

Beauty of

Maryland

Text: James F. Waesche

Concept & Design: Robert D. Shangle

Revised Edition
First Printing October, 1991
Published by LTA Publishing Company
2735 S.E. Raymond Street, Portland, Oregon 97202
Robert D. Shangle, Publisher

"Learn about America in a beautiful way."

This book features the photography of
James Blank
Robert Shangle
Shangle Photographics

Library of Congress Cataloging-in-Publication Data
Waesche, James F.
    Beauty of Maryland / text, James F. Waesche.
        p.   cm.
    Revised edition of: Beautiful Maryland / concept and design, Robert D. Shangle;
text, James F. Waesche. c1980.
    ISBN 1-55988-037-6 (hardbound): $19.95. — ISBN 1-55988-036-8 (paperback):
$9.95
    1. Maryland — Description and travel — 1981 — Views. 2. Maryland — Descrip-
tion and travel — 1981 — Guide-books. I. Title.
F182.W34   1991
917.504'43 — dc20   91-26988
                                                                                  CIP

Production, Concept and Distribution by LTA Publishing Company, Portland, Oregon.
Printed in Thailand. This book produced as the major component of the "World Peace and
Understanding" program of Beauty of America Printing Company, Portland, Oregon.

Contents

The Maryland Mix

The point of land is one of many that jut into the broad Potomac River from St. Mary's, Maryland's mother country.

It is a thickly wooded point, its leafy green mass bordered by a narrow beach of glistening white sand. Only a few gnarled abstractions of sun-bleached driftwood bristle up from the wavelet-smoothed strand.

The river at this point is only a few miles from its confluence with the storied Chesapeake Bay. It is wide and quiet here, and its waters lap the beach gently, as though the river is satisfied that it has nearly reached its destination.

Over the soft rhythm of the wavelets' lapping can be heard the intermittent calls of gulls and land birds, the whisperings of breeze-stirred leaves and pine needles. Nowhere is there the sound of man . . . nowhere at all.

In the distance a button of color pops over the horizon. Bright red and yellow, it balances lightly on the line that separates river from sky. Even at this distance, most observers would immediately recognize it as a spinnaker that's no doubt pulling a yacht of no mean dimensions.

But the *romantic* observer — that individual who can suspend his sense of time and let his imagination dance — such an observer can see not a ballooning spinnaker, but, instead, the square, grey-white sails of the ship *Ark*, one of the two tiny vessels that deposited Maryland's founding colonists on these St. Mary's shores in 1635.

The vision is really quite easy to conjure, for very little along this part of the Potomac has changed in Maryland's three and a half centuries of history.

What's even more miraculous is this: the scene, the setting, are not unique. Spots of similar serenity, of similar changelessness, can be found along other St. Mary's points and coves.

Miraculous?

The non-Marylander has a right to be incredulous — until he is informed that these calm, lovely, and seemingly timeless spots are only 50 miles as the seagull flies from Washington, D.C. They are even closer to the clover-leaves, parking lots, shopping centers, and drive-in-every-things that serve the capital's sprawling suburbs.

The D.C. suburbs are just as much a part of today's Maryland as are the reminders of Maryland's yesterdays. As such, they are merely the latest in a series of changes that have altered the state over the decades and the centuries. Always these two aspects of Maryland — the old and the unspoiled on the one hand, the new and progressive on the other — have run collision courses. Such collisions are inevitable in many places in the United States. Maryland, though, is particularly vulnerable to them because Maryland is such an old state. And because it is small: only 10,577 square miles — and that includes 703 square miles of water!

Within that small area mix the dynamics that so often clash. Maryland, that is to say, is both densely urban and sparsely rural. It is both highly industrial and technocratic, yet it is also productively agricultural. Tobacco is still grown, as it has been since the 17th century — yet not far from the tobacco fields, more than 1,000 scientists at the U.S. Department of Agriculture's Research Center experiment with the crops of the future. On the Chesapeake Bay, men dredge for oysters in sturdy sailboats, the last fleet of working sail in the country — yet through the wakes of these antique boats ply the modern ships of commerce that make the city of Baltimore one of the busiest ports on the Atlantic Coast.

This dynamic "Maryland mix" is evidence of a thriving economy. Inherent in it, however, is that age-old potential for conflict. Shall urban or industrial or commercial expansion be permitted at the expense of natural or historic or agricultural preservation? Shall efforts toward such preservation stifle or thwart economic growth?

The Lay of The Land

Although Maryland is indeed a small state, it possesses an amazing natural diversity: mountainous highlands, gently rolling Piedmont farmlands, tidewater flatlands, and broad sandy shores washed by the Atlantic Ocean. In Maryland's westernmost county is a sub-Arctic swamp that contains the continent's southernmost growth of tamarack. And in Maryland are the East Coast's two northernmost stands of bald cypress.

By far the larger of the two cypress forests is the one which grows along the murky banks of the Pocomoke River. Canoeing on this mysteriously dark river, one is overcome by the scent of wild magnolias, the sight of stately herons and egrets, and by glimpses of iridescent dragonflies darting from one water lily blossom to another.

If atypical of Maryland rivers, the Pocomoke is thoroughly typical of the state's natural scenery. It is peaceful, tranquil. It reveals itself quietly, with subtlety and charm; it does not overwhelm with drama.

Maryland's beauty is not manifest exclusively in natural form. Because it is also an old state — truly ancient on this country's time scale — many of its most pleasing sights are man-made, man-made in eras when aesthetics were more important than budget print-outs, and in eras when growth was organic and linked to the land (or, in Maryland's case, to the water).

The diversity that characterizes Maryland's natural attractions characterizes its man-made ones as well. Whereas eminently civilized Georgian mansions command tiered green hillsides overlooking Maryland's tidal rivers, frontier houses of stone — houses that are more fort than home — still guard their rocky Western Maryland premises. Whitecottaged fishing villages which have embraced quiet coves and harbors for 300 years demand comparison with the planned squares and formal façades of such 18th century towns as Annapolis and Chestertown and Frederick. Likewise, the proud monuments and carefully planned garden suburbs of Baltimore, the state's largest city, stand in sharp contrast to the tiny towns of Western Maryland, whose tree-shaded Main Streets are casually lined with tri-colored houses: red brick walls, white trim, green shutters and roofs.

But long before Maryland's historic and cultural landmarks took shape, there was the land itself. As a land mass, the state so many think of as primarily coastal is firmly rooted in the Appalachian Mountains. In fact, the wild white waters of the Youghiogheny, a river in Maryland's western-most county, don't flow across the eastern seaboard at all. Instead of heading east, the Yough turns its back on the rest of Maryland and seeks first the Monongahela, then the Ohio, and finally the Mississippi. Eventually, water that bubbled to life from some Maryland spring winds up in the Gulf of Mexico!

Actually, Maryland's Appalachian Province is tri-partite, the Youghiogheny's drainage area being the highest (generally over 3,000 feet above sea level) and the farthest from the ocean. It is a region of coal, this land of northward flowing streams, and it is a region of farms for the raising of wheat and corn, barley and oats; of pastures for the grazing of cattle and sheep; and of forests for the making of sweet maple syrup and sugar.

In the vicinity of Cumberland, the land drops a bit in elevation, and the terrain crinkles into a corrugation of narrow ridges and valleys. Here, thin soil and sharply rising ridge walls restrict farming. Scenery, however, is another matter entirely. New vistas and panoramas unfold as roads hair-pin up and down the sides of the mountains.

When the roads dip low, travelers will be taken through quiet hollows where the sound of the car may frighten into flight a scarlet cardinal, a rabbit, or a deer. When the roads ride high, the views will encompass the horizon. In good weather one can see for miles, often into other states. In summer, the nearest slopes will be a bright, luminous green; the farthest, pale grey-blue. Clouds will drag splotches of shade across the hillsides, and, occasionally, a distant cabin will send a twist of smoke into the sky. At twilight, darkness will begin to suck up the space between the ridges and the mountains will go flat, becoming like grey cardboard cutouts pasted one behind the other. In autumn, of course, the hills blaze with the colors that characterize Eastern deciduous forests: red and sienna, gold and vivid pure-yellow.

In any season, keen observers will note that the profiles of Maryland's mountains are low; the peaks not usually peaked at all, but, rather, softly rounded or even level, like loaves of bread. This leveling has come about only after the passage of an unimaginable period of time, for the Appalachians are among the earth's oldest mountains. Once higher and craggier than the Rockies (those geological upstarts of the West), the East's Appalachians have been worn and eroded, submerged and exposed, over countless eons. The mountains visible today, therefore, are merely the remnants, the roots, as it were — of once-towering formations.

One of the most impressive sites in this middle zone of Maryland's Appalachian Province is Cumberland Narrows, a deep gap in the mountains cut by Wills Creek, a tributary of the Potomac. The craggy walls of the mile-long gorge rise sharply from the rock-strewn stream to a height of some 800 feet.

From the high and furrowed terrain of Allegany and western Washington County, mountainous Maryland dips to form the Cumberland (or Hagerstown) Valley, this state's portion of the great trough that runs for a thousand miles through the entire Appalachian chain. Underlain by limestone rocks that bespeak a time when the region was beneath the sea, Cumberland Valley is amazingly fertile, supporting large prosperous grain and dairy farms.

The eastern wall of the Valley is South Mountain, only 1,100 feet high. It is as though Maryland has tired of the ordeal of making mountains, for east of South Mountain she thrusts up only one final chain, the gentle Catoctins, on whose hills spread forests of black locust, wild cherry, oak, and sassafras.

East of the mountains Maryland's descent to the sea continues across the Piedmont Plateau, a region that comprises about one-quarter of the state's land area. Here, horses hunt to hounds across lush, white-fenced valleys; beef cattle graze by brooks that wind through the greenest of pastures; rivers whose headwaters are Appalachian or foothill springs meander through forest and field to their tidal transmutations at the Fall Line, that abrupt change in land-level and topography that defines the boundary between the hilly, rocky Piedmont Plateau and the level, sandy-gravelly Coastal Plain.

Geologically speaking, the Coastal Plain is Maryland's youngest region. Sedimentary in character, it is composed of deposits laid down by the ocean as it alternately advanced and retreated over the millenia.

Clear proof of the Plain's sedimentary nature lies bared for all to see at Calvert Cliffs, a 35-mile stretch of sheer, sandy precipice that rises from the Chesapeake Bay along the eastern shoreline of Calvert County. Over 190 feet high in places, the cliffs reveal stratum upon stratum of silt and fossils dating from the Miocene Period — dating, in other words, from some ten or 15 million years ago, when the Plain lay beneath the sea. Today, amateur and professional geologists delight in trekking along the cliffs to probe for fossilized remnants of sharks, crocodiles, mastodons, and whales.

Most of Maryland's Coastal Plain, however, is nowhere near as high above sea level as are the Calvert Cliffs. No, most of the Plain lies low, daring not to rise far above the sea that gave it birth. Much, in fact, is marshland — if, indeed, the boggy marshes' tufts of pickerelweed, wild rice, and Olney three-square can be called land.

A desolate and lonely beauty have these marshes, these vast expanses of demi-land. Here the leafless branches and gaunt trunks of salt-tainted pines form the only verticals in an otherwise horizontal world where sky presses flat upon a mosaic of shallow ponds, twisting tidal streams, and mucky land.

The best time to see a marsh is during an autumn sunset. During the high daylight hours, the reflections of clouds and pines in the blue-green waters of the marshes will have been intriguing. At sunset, however, the display is gripping.

As the sun begins to drop, it tints the tall grasses gold. The gold slowly deepens to russet, and the sun, swollen and heavy with redness, streaks the sky as it falls closer and closer to the water. Across the vivid streaks sweep noisily honking vees of Canadian Geese, returning from their day of feeding in inland grain fields.

Finally the sun reaches the horizon. For a moment it rests there, flattening into an oval as it pauses. Then it breaks through. It plunges into the waters and dissolves, releasing torrents of color into the countless ponds and guts of the marsh.

The color floats until it's drawn off by the grasses, which turn slightly rose. Then, within an hour, the pale rose is absorbed, the marsh is pitch dark, and its winged denizens are quiet with sleep.

If marshes can be places of beauty, they definitely are places of vital importance to the ecology of the Chesapeake system. They provide cover and food for waterfowl and other birds, for mammals such as the muskrat, which lives exclusively within their watery confines, and for fish, crabs, and other aquatic life. Just as important, as the marshes' grasses die and decompose, they return needed nutrients to the entire system. A marsh, then, only seems to be an empty expanse of bleak desolation. In truth, it is a cradle of life.

Marshes are found not only along the Chesapeake itself, but also along Maryland's oceanside bays: the Sinepuxent, the Chincoteague, and the Assawoman. These marshes do not, however, form the state's coastal margin. That margin, that final edge of Maryland that slips beneath the waves of the Atlantic Ocean, is a 30-mile-long strip of sandy beaches and dunes that runs roughly north-south between the coastal bays and the ocean. Although it carries upon its narrow spine both resort and park (Ocean City and Assateague, respectively), this barrier island, this coastal sandbar, is not as stable a piece of real estate as those developments would suggest.

Less than a mile wide in spots, the island is a product not of earthly upheavals of solid rock and stone, but, rather, of the pulses of the ever-changing sea. In living memory, inlets have been closed and opened by the action of surf and tide. Even now the island wanders — shifts east or west — as waves either toss up sand or claw it away.

Chesapeake Bay

Separating the mountains from the sea — yet, in a very real sense drawing them together by means of its far-flowing tributaries — is the Chesapeake Bay, the largest estuary in the United States. One hundred and ninety-five miles long from its head, at the mouths of the Susquehanna and Elk Rivers in upper Maryland, to its mouth at Cape Charles and Henry in Virgina, the Bay proper covers an area of 3,237 square miles. More than half that area lies within Maryland. Varying in width from three to 20 miles, it is in spots up to 175 feet deep. But that's only in spots, for the Bay, considering its size, is surprisingly shallow; it averages only 27.6 feet.

As bodies of water go, the Chesapeake is relatively young, being only between 15,000 to 18,000 years old. Much earlier, what is now the Bay was an extension of the Susquehanna River. With the last melting of the polar ice caps, however, rising seas backed into and literally flooded the Susquehanna's lower segment. They overflowed not only the ancient river channel itself, but also large areas of the land surrounding it. In a very real sense, the Chesapeake Bay is a "drowned river."

Today, many other rivers in addition to the Susquehanna contribute to the Bay. Their names . . . Choptank, Patapsco, Patuxent, Chester, Tred Avon, Miles . . . bespeak the state's Indian and British heritages. Their fresh water, merging and mixing with the saline surges from the ocean, creates a remarkably congenial blend for a vast array of life forms. And their shorelines, added to those of the Bay itself, give little Maryland a total tidal shoreline (albeit an incredibly convoluted one) of some 4,000 miles. When one realizes that Baltimore City and 16 of 23 counties border this tidal system, one can begin to understand the Chesapeake's significance to a state the size of Maryland.

Most obvious, perhaps, the Bay presents itself as an exceedingly hospitable habitat for commercially important fin and shellfish. Herring, shad, white and yellow perch, the tasty striped bass (called "rock" in Maryland), hard- and soft-shelled clams, bluefish, blue crabs, and the justly famed oyster constitute important elements of the great Chesapeake fishery.

Although some of the Bay's abundant produce is taken by sophisticated mechanical means (as an example, long vacuum-equipped conveyor belts suck succulent soft-shelled clams from their bay-bottom beds), much is still obtained largely by means used long ago. Take the case of oysters, of which Maryland is the nation's leading provider. Although an increasing number of watermen are using mechanical patent tongs, many of their brothers still laboriously tug the delectible bivalves out of the water with long, back-breaking hand tongs. Others choose still to use sharp-toothed metal dredges which are dragged over the oyster beds by those working sailboats we mentioned earlier.

Called skipjacks, these wooden boats have shallow vee-bottoms and single masts sharply raked. They are 19th century descendants of the smaller bateaux built by colonists in the 17th century for crabbing, hunting, and, even then, for oystering.

A skipjack's hull is invariably white; its two sails (a mainsail and a jib) are of varying intensities of weathered grey, depending on their age. Hand-carved, brightly painted trailboards affixed beneath the bowsprits and bearing their boat's name, give a skipjack its only flashes of color.

To observe a skipjack in action, its sails taut in the wind, to watch as its cap'n uses the knowledge of generations to guide it over the invisible oyster beds below . . . to see this is to see one of this mechanized, "sophisticated" society's few remaining examples of man's age-old, face-to-face struggle with nature for his livelihood.

As one would suspect, the Chesapeake's value to Maryland and to Marylanders does not stem solely from the commercial fishery it supports. Curving as it does along the southern third or so of Megalopolis, northeast America's "super city," the Chesapeake is a watery playground for the populations of Philadelphia, Wilmington, Baltimore, and Washington — especially for the yachtsmen among them.

Marinas and sailing clubs pepper the Bay's shores. In some cases, entire towns have become yachting centers. Two such are picturesque Oxford and St. Michaels, in Talbot County, where it's said that no spot of land is more than five miles from water. Georgetown on the beautiful Sassafras River is another. Queen of them all is Annapolis.

Annapolis is Maryland's capital; it is the proud possessor of more superb 18th century buildings than any other place in the once-English colonies; since 1845 it has been home of the U.S. Naval Academy. But during the sailing season, Annapolis becomes to many people the very center of the universe. It is from here, after all, that the prestigious Annapolis-to-Bermuda and Annapolis-to-Newport races are run. During these and other height-of-season highlights, even the town's cramped 300-year-old commercial harbor takes in as many pleasure boats as it can. There they moor, amidst clam rigs, excursion boats, crabbers, and maybe a skipjack or two. From the water, a tapestry of masts and spars almost obscures the gleaming white dome of Maryland's 1770's State House. From the land, from the streets of town, those same swaying masts are like an array of arms beckoning, tempting the observer to yield to the lure of the Bay and the sea beyond.

There is yet another aspect of the Chesapeake's significance to Maryland: it is the great highway that carries international commerce to and from the Port of Baltimore, Tankers, container ships, and freighters ply its channels in such number that they enable the Port to generate fully one-tenth of Maryland's gross state product. Though these floating giants contribute next to naught to the *beauty* of Maryland, their absence from state waters, and from its economy, would be unthinkable.

Of course, it should be admitted that a certain romance surrounds even these monster-ships, these carriers of goods among the world's most exotic seaports. That romance can make itself felt with special pungence in the colonial-era Fells Point section of Baltimore, where the great ships tie up at end-of-street docks and loom over the nearby taverns and chandleries with awesome bulk. It can also be felt in the 19th century canal town of Chesapeake City, which sits alongside the Chesapeake and Delaware Canal.

Fort McHenry, Baltimore

Baltimore Skyline and Inner Harbor

Lock 20, Chesapeake and Ohio Canal

United States Naval Academy, Annapolis

St. Mary's City

Oxford Ferry, Talbot County

Cunningham Falls State Park

Civil War-War Correspondents Memorial, Gathland State Park

Burnside Bridge, Antietam National Battlefield

Boat Harbor, Annapolis

North of Kingsville

Great Falls Tavern

Sailing off Fort McHenry

St. Michaels, Talbot County

Owens Creek, Catoctin Mountain Park

Great Falls of the Potomac

Brookside Gardens, Wheaton

Tom Johnson Bridge

Johns Hopkins University

First Memorial to George Washington, Washington Monument State Park

St. Michaels

Sandy Point State Park

William Paca House and Garden, Annapolis

Ocean City

Maryland Farm Country, Montgomery County

Blackwater National Wildlife Refuge, Dorchester County

Assateague Island Lighthouse

Hampton House National Historic Site

Baltimore's Inner Harbor

Pumpkin Time in Talbot County

Monocacy Aqueduct, Dickerson

Le Dew Topiary Garden, near Hess

United States Naval Academy, Annapolis

Point of Rocks Railway Station

Kettering Community Park, Prince George's County

Grist Mill at Susquehana State Park

Point Lookout

Drum Point Lighthouse, Calvert County

Old City Hall, Salisbury

North of Broomes Island

Antietam National Battlefield

Assateague Bay, Worchester County

Utica Covered Bridge near Lewistown

Evergreen House, Baltimore

Tolliver Falls, Swallow Falls State Park

Casselman Bridge State Park, Grantsville

State Capitol Building, Annapolis

Choptank River

As its name implies, the canal connects the Delaware River, just below Wilmington, with the upper Chesapeake. Carrying more traffic than the Panama Canal, the C & D is a vital route to and from the Port of Baltimore. Chesapeake City is interesting in itself — because of its decayed-boomtown atmosphere and because of the restored 1837 pump house on its outskirts. But it is the ships themselves that are most evocative, especially at night when their black, ill-defined silhouettes blot out the lights on the opposite shore and they take on whatever identity their observer's imagination wishes to give them.

Tidewater Maryland

The Chesapeake has always played a preeminent role in the life of Maryland. Although Italian explorers are thought to have set foot in the state's Atlantic shore, it was the Chesapeake Bay that was the real trunk of exploration, settlement, and commerce.

The colony began in 1634 near that sandy riverbank in St. Mary's County, about 15 miles up from the mouth of the Potomac. The settlement was christened St. Mary's City, but a true city it never was and never would be. As recent archeological excavations have revealed, St. Mary's was never much more than a country village, even in its 17th century heyday. Still, it did represent the beginning, and beginnings deserve to be commemorated.

Maryland honored its beginning in 1934 — on the 300th anniversary of the colony's founding — by the construction of a replica of the State House that was originally raised at St. Mary's in 1676. Today, the two-storied, cruciform building stands in lonely splendor near the bank of the St. Mary's River. How tiny and unassuming it seems to us — but how imposing it must have been when it towered above the little half-timbered dwellings that lined long-vanished Aldermanbery Street.

There is, though, an authentic "early Maryland" view at St. Mary's. It focuses upon the river's far shore, where on a knoll of cleared ground stands West St. Mary's Manor, an early 18th century brick-ended house that displays the double chimneys so characteristic of its place and period.

From the St. Mary's settlement, colonization spread throughout Tidewater Maryland. It did not spread via overland routes, because they were few and primitive. Bogs, dense virgin forests, and temperamental streams made road-building impractical. But there was really little need to worry about roads in a region blessed with the Chesapeake and its many tributaries — tributaries that reached far into the interior of the colony. It was along these paths of least resistance that development did occur.

It occurred not in the form of towns, as was the pattern in the New England colonies, but in the form of plantations, which were nearly self-sufficient social and economic units, tied tightly to the mother country by ship-borne lines of trade and credit.

Commanding these estates were the houses of the planters. Not all of them were the pillared, pedimented mansions of which movies and nostalgia are made. But many were — especially those built in the 18th rather than the 17th century — and many still stand.

Few, unfortunately, are easily seen. Like most everything else in colonial Maryland, they were oriented toward the water. So they remain. Sailors can catch glimpses of their warm brick façades, their balanced wings, classical white porticoes, and terraced lawns. For the most part, however, landlubbers must await the house and garden tours that highlight Maryland springs, early summers, and falls.

Happily, there are a few plantation houses that are open to the public. Mt. Clare, its view of the Patapsco River now obliterated by some of Baltimore City's heavy industry, is one. Sotterley, displaying magnificent woodwork and furnishings, beautifully situated on the Patuxent River, is another. Baltimore County's Hampton is a third.

But to get a truly good suggestion of what 18th century plantation life was like — as good a one, that is, as one can get nowadays — one can drive past Doughregan Manor, in Howard County. One can drive past, but one can't get in, for this place is still a working farm very privately in the hands of descendants of its original builders. Stables, barns, and erstwhile slave quarters still surround this immensely impressive survival of Maryland's colonial past.

It is Annapolis, of course, that is Maryland's treasure chest of colonial architecture. It abounds with great houses that differ from their country cousins only in their city locations. Finely restored and lovingly maintained, a number of them are open to the public.

Behind one, the 35-room Paca House, blooms one of the finest gardens in all Maryland. Covering some two acres, the garden's formal *falles*, or terraces, drop down from the mansion's stairtower to an informal area dominated by a placid pond. Interestingly, the garden is as exact a replica of William Paca's own 18th century garden as 20th century archaeology and horticulture can create. Its roses, shrubs, perennials, herbs, and "roots" are all varieties that would have been available in the 1760s, and the placements of its parterres, Chippendale footbridge, gazebo, and *grande allée* are based on documentary or excavated evidence.

Paca, Ogle, Hammond-Harwood, Dulaney, Chase-Lloyd . . . The names of the Annapolis mansions comprise a register of Maryland's wealthy late-colonial oligarchy, an oligarchy whose fortunes were made from a variety of endeavors: the growing, milling and sale of wheat and other grains; money-lending and finance; land speculation, and industrial investment. (For a while, the smelting of iron was particularly lucrative. The ruins of one of the largest of the colonial furnace complexes are visible at Principio, in Cecil County.)

Maryland's earliest fortunes, however, had had a different source. They had sprouted from the soil in the form of tobacco.

Tobacco is still cultivated in Southern Maryland, those counties that lie south of Washington, D.C., between the Chesapeake on the east and the Potomac on the southwest. Strangers to the land of tobacco can quickly recognize the fields in which it's grown even when they can't recognize the tall, broad-leafed sotweed itself. The fields are distinguished by their unique barns: wooden buildings with slatted or louvered sides. (These slats can be swung open to allow air to enter. Over a period of time, the circulating air dries, or *cures*, the tobacco leaves that hang inside.)

Until the growth of Baltimore in the immediate post-Revolutionary period, and until the sprawl of Washington, which shows no signs of abating even today, Maryland was a rural, agricultural state. Of course there were towns — trading centers, tobacco and wheat ports, governmental centers. So busy and glittering was 18th century Annapolis, in fact, that it was called the "Athens of America." But Maryland's "urban" centers were not New Yorks, Philadelphias, or Bostons. So much the better, perhaps, because today many of the early towns that remain are still small, human-scaled, and slow of pace — thoroughly delightful places, in other words.

Some of the towns, needless to say, haven't remained, at least as such. Old St. Mary's is under the ground, in less than ruins. Port Tobacco, its river having silted up long ago, is a handful of houses — albeit lovely ones — and a restored courthouse. Georgetown, not the aforementioned Georgetown on the Sassafras, but the Georgetown on the Potomac, now exists merely as a swanky residential section within the limits of the District of Columbia. In the 18th century it was one of Maryland's busiest ports, tapping some of the grain-rich hinterlands whose produce was later siphoned away by Baltimore.

The Eastern Shore

Of the towns that have lasted, many of the most appealing are to be found on the Eastern Shore, that distinctive portion of Maryland that lies east of the Chesapeake Bay and shares the Delmarva Peninsula with Delaware and two counties of Virginia. Almost entirely surrounded by water, the peninsula was by-passed by the forces of growth once the country's major modes of transportation became propelled by internal combustion and diesel engines rather than sails and paddle wheels.

Like Princess Anne on the Manokin River, for instance, or like Snow Hill on the cypress-lined Pocomoke, some Eastern Shore towns have survived primarily because they are county seats. Oxford and St. Michaels, as we have said, have been resurrected as yachting centers. Not, of course, that these two don't have other appeals as well. Oxford, its tree-lined streets bordered by white picket fences and brick sidewalks laid in herringbone patterns, is a terminus of what's thought to be the country's oldest privately operated ferry; it was launched in 1683. St. Michael's is home of the Chesapeake Bay Maritime Museum, the repository of an authentic screw-pile lighthouse, a peculiar, spider-legged affair of a type that aided Chesapeake Bay navigation for generations.

Then too, there are Chestertown and Easton, both old, gracious, and picturesque; both county seats. Chestertown is also a college town, the site of Washington College, on whose board of governors sat George himself. Easton is the boutique-y "shopping center" of Talbot and Queen Anne's Counties.

But there exists on the Eastern Shore another, entirely different, breed of town. These are fishing villages. More than any of Maryland's other contemporary communities, they offer direct views into by-gone days, views only slightly skewed by the passing of time.

The names of these communities say a lot about their orientation: Taylor's *Island*, Deal *Island*, Hooper's *Island*, Tilghman *Island*, Smith *Island*. (Don't, though, go generalizing about Chesapeake Bay islands. Gibson Island, at the mouth of the Magothy on the Western Shore, is a very posh, very clubby, very private retreat of Baltimore's Old Families. To see that it remains just that way, guards are posted at the narrow causeway that links the island to the rest of Maryland.)

Of the "fishing islands," Smith is the most remote and, largely because of its remoteness, the quintessential. Maryland's southernmost community, it rises, barely, from Tangier Sound 11 miles east of Crisfield, the Somerset County town long known as "The Seafood Capital of the World."

Smith Island's population lives in three villages: Ewell, Rhodes Point, or Tylertown. Each village is a cluster of white frame houses lent color by hollyhocks and marigolds, pink-blossomed mimosa trees, and bountiful vegetable gardens. Each village also has its own stubby-steepled little church.

But it is neither churches nor houses that stand out as the most distinctive structures of Smith Island. No, its most distinctive structures are the weathered crab shanties built on the ends of the dozens of wooden piers that thrust out into the innumerable guts, channels, and "thoroughfares" that interlace to make Smith Island a sort of rustic Venice.

Inside the shanties are the worktables where crabs are packed for shipment to Crisfield. Outside, floating in fenced-off "pounds," are rows of liveboxes, raftlike affairs with slats for sides so water can flow in and out. In these boxes hard crabs are confined while they shed their shells. Once they have, they are, logically, soft crabs, one of the most prized of the Chesapeake's many delicacies.

The rickety, rafty geometries of Smith Island's piers and shanties, of its irregular stacks of wire-mesh crabpots, are enlivened by the movement of boats . . . small rowboats used for tending liveboxes and considerably longer boats used for actual deep water crabbing.

As one moves inland on the Eastern Shore, one passes from a maritime to an agricultural economy; away from small fishing villages to not-much-larger towns that serve as gathering, processing, and distribution centers for the produce of the countryside immediately surrounding them. That produce might be tomatoes or corn, soybeans or wheat, eggs or poultry. Because the towns are usually old and therefore architecturally interesting, they serve as pleasant respites from the rather boring sameness of the flat farmlands that spread across the Eastern Shore's interior.

We have noted that the peninsula Eastern Shore was "Bypassed by progress" once waterways ceased to be prime bearers of transportation and commerce. That cessation — that shift in the means and routes of movement — was a slow, gradual process. Its beneficiary was Maryland's present-day metropolis, Baltimore.

Baltimore and the West

Like so many other Maryland towns, Baltimore had its start as a to-bacco port. But Baltimore had several advantages not possessed by its competitors: its location on the relatively deep Patapsco; its situation directly upon the Fall Line; and its command of a vast, fertile hinterland which embraced not only the western counties of Maryland, but also parts of south-central Pennsylvania and northern Virginia. In those areas, wheat, not tobacco, was king.

With all those wheatfields to draw upon, with readily available stream-power to grind it into flour, and with a deep-water port from which to ship either the grain or the flour, Baltimore rapidly grew from "just another" tidewater port of entry to one of the young nation's largest cities.

To ever-expand their city's trading position, Baltimoreans estab-lished financial institutions, laid westward-bound highways, conceived and built the famed Baltimore clippers, and, most ingenious of all, laid the country's first commercial railroad. Naturally, the railroad headed west.

In late 20th century Baltimore there are many reminders of the glory-days of the early 19th. Moored in the city's splendidly renewed Inner Harbor is the *Pride of Baltimore*, an exact replica of one of the early fortune-building clippers. Only a few blocks away stands Mount Clare Sta-tion, the oldest railroad passenger depot in the world, and an adjacent roundhouse that contains the B & O Railroad Museum's impressive collec-tion of historic locomotives and other railroad memorabilia.

Also visible in and near Baltimore are vestiges of early milling cen-ters. Rockland Mill and two rows of little stone houses stand just north of the city in Brooklandville. Other stone millhouses line the banks of Jones Falls, a stream that flows through the city from the north. And beside still another stream, near the hilly, forested parkland of western Baltimore, is Dickeyville, which looks for all the world as though it had been transplanted directly from New England.

Some of the wealth created in young Baltimore was directed into the foundation of the great institutions that still enrich the metropolitan area's life, institutions whose names perpetuate the names of their founders: the Walters Art Gallery, the Enoch Pratt Free Library, the Peabody Institute and Conservatory of Music, Goucher College, the Johns Hopkins University and Hospital . . .

Not surprisingly, some of that wealth also found its way into the construction of grand mansions. Several still adorn the Baltimore cityscape.

The finest distillation of Baltimore's age of philanthropy and elegant living can be found in Mt. Vernon Place, the four-armed square whose focal point is a towering monument to George Washington. Called one of the most beautiful urban spaces in America, Mt. Vernon Place is resplendent with conservatory, library, art gallery, spired church, private clubs, townhouses and apartments. Each building is handsomely designed; each is harmoniously situated and proportioned with regard to its neighbors.

Elsewhere too in Baltimore are places of surprising appeal: Fort McHenry, proudly flying the "Star-Spangled Banner" from a spearhead of land that pokes defiantly into the Patapsco; Sherwood Gardens, a springtime splendor of tulips and azaleas; the gleaming new office towers which rise alongside the Inner Harbor; the restoration-conscious colonial neighborhood of Fells Point; and Federal Hill, a high green eminence that overlooks the city's Inner Harbor and downtown skyline.

It is from the top of Federal Hill that one can truly understand the nature of Baltimore as a port and the role it played in the westward growth of Maryland, and, indeed, of the country itself.

To the southeast flows the Patapsco, out to the Chesapeake and finally to the ocean. To the west rise the hills that are the heralds of Piedmont, the first steps along the route that eventually leads to Midwestern grainfields and America's industrial heartland. It was the Midwest toward which the earliest highways and railroads pushed out from Baltimore.

The direct descendants of the most important of the roads west are Maryland's Route 144 and US 40, the former older than the latter, as they intertwine and overlap up the countryside between Baltimore City and Western Maryland.

Parts of the road — just west of Cumberland, for instance, follow old Indian trails. Still other sections were surveyed as military routes. (In 1755, the forces of General Edward Braddock hacked through primeval forest on the way to their ill-fated attack on Fort Duquesne, now Pittsburgh.) The route as a whole, however, finally materialized because it was commercially and politically necessary to link the East Coast with America's ever-expanding western frontier.

The most famous of those latter segments was the National or Cumberland Road, the first public works project ever authorized by the U.S. Congress. Approval of the project was granted in 1806, three years after the Louisiana Purchase attached the mid-Continent to the eastern seaboard. Work began in Cumberland. In 1821, the road reached the Ohio River at Wheeling, West Virgina, then Virginia. (By that time, yet another section, called the Bank Road because it was supported by Baltimore and Western Maryland financial institutions, had been completed between Baltimore and Cumberland.)

Tracing this historic route one comes to Ellicott City, only 12 miles from Baltimore. Although this town is now the seat of rapidly suburbanizing Howard County, it originally developed around one of the grist and flour mills that contributed so much to the port of Baltimore, and around the first depot built outside Baltimore by the B & O Railroad.

That 1830 depot still stands, as do many of the town's early houses and shops. Though constructed of dark granite sliced out of nearby quarries, they seem to have grown from the sides of the rocky cleft through which the old road squeezes. Many of the vintage buildings have been adapted to new uses. They are antique shops, boutiques, bistros. Still, because of their period style and solid construction, the presence of the past lingers forcefully in Ellicott City.

As it goes farther west, the road passes New Market, an old stage-stop town that's now an antique center, before coming to Frederick.

Frederick is one of those "either-or" places. Depending on how one approaches it, and on one's point of view, Frederick is either the western-most of Maryland's colonial Tidewater towns or the easternmost of its mountain towns. Regardless of the label one decides to attach to it, Frederick is a place of considerable charm and beauty.

> "Up from the meadows rich with corn,
> Clear in the cool September morn,
> The clustered spires of Frederick stand
> Green-walled by the hills of Maryland."

So wrote poet John Greenleaf Whittier in the last century. So he could write today, for those self-same "clustered spires" still dominate the Frederick skyline. In their shadows, along this gracious town's grid-ironed streets, are rows and squares of red brick Federal townhouses set off with immaculate white trim, wrought-iron fences, and highly polished brass fixtures.

If those poetized spires dominate Frederick the town, Frederick the county has its comparable "spire" in Sugarloaf Mountain, a geological anomaly that pokes 1,300 feet above the bank of the Potomac River near Frederick County's boundary with Montgomery County. Discovered by a Swiss explorer in 1707, the solitary peak can be climbed via designated walking paths. The views of the Potomac valley from Sugarloaf's top are well worth the effort of the climb.

Sugarloaf is an anomaly because the mountains proper are to the west, not the southeast, of Frederick. The first of the ranges is formed by the Catoctin Mountains, many of whose crests lie within either the Catoctin Mountain National Park or the Cunningham Falls State Park.

Secluded and well-guarded within the national park is Camp David, the presidential retreat established by Franklin Roosevelt and maintained by every U.S. president since. Most of the park, however, is accessible to the public. Hiking trails lace through it and the state reservation, through forests of chestnut, oak, hickory, and black birch. Scenic overlooks open among the trees that grow on the heights; cool, clear trout streams flow among those that shade the hollows.

Rising one valley west of the Catoctin parks is South Mountain.

Atop its rocky summit stands an historical oddity, a squat structure that resembles a huge, truncated beehive. The strange stone thing is nothing less, however, than the first monument ever erected in honor of George Washington. Built in a single day (July 4, appropriately, in the year 1827) by several hundred patriotic citizens of nearby Boonsboro, it commands views of parts of Maryland, Pennsylvania, West Virginia, and Virginia.

Close by, also on South Mountain, is yet another unusual monument, this one a considerably more sophisticated affair of arched and turret brick. Dedicated to the memory of Civil War newspaper correspondents, it is the world's only monument to a free press. Since it is in a clearing that is quite close to the Appalachian trail, its high Victorian elaborateness has no doubt presented something of a shock to unsuspecting hikers who come suddenly upon it as they emerge from the surrounding forest.

From the Catoctins roughly to that point west of Hagerstown where Maryland pinches to a width of only 1.9 miles, the mountains rise gently and elevations are relatively low. Between the ridges are rich valleys that nurture orchards of apples and peaches, pastures where dairy cattle browse, and fields of wheat and corn.

Amid the fields are large brick-ended barns that sit sturdily on high stone foundations. Silos nestle comfortably against them. The commodious houses nearby, often also of stone, spread wide, welcoming porches across their fronts. Together, the structures arrange themselves into very satisfying compositions of mass, volume, and texture.

But in these Western Maryland farms one finds more than pleasing compositions. One finds expressions of a certain honesty, a certain time-proved harmony between man and the land that sustains him. Streams follow their natural courses. Green rows of crops and red-brown furrows of newly-turned earth sweep around hillsides in broad contours. Wings of houses bear testimony not to attempt to out-do the Joneses, but to what until recently was simply the natural scheme of things: the marriage of a son or daughter; the birth of a child; the arrival of a new generation, one that would inherit and repeat the pattern. It all engenders feelings of peace, of people at ease with the land and with each other.

Such was not always the case.

In the early 1860s, the War Between the States swept back and forth, north and south, through these gentle Maryland valleys. Skirmishes were fought. Battles were waged. Whole towns were held for ransom. Thousands of young men died. In the annals of the war in Maryland, no name was writ with bloodier ink than was the name Antietam.

Only a creek actually, one of several that meander through the Western Maryland valleys on their way to the Potomac River, the Antietam in September of 1862 became the site of the goriest of the war's battles. Today the place is tranquil — but eerily so, because the fields around are filled with monuments and cannon and knobby limestone outcroppings the color of gravestones. Under Burnside Bridge, itself the object of intense fighting between Blue and Grey, Antietam Creek murmurs on, giving not a hint that one day long ago its waters ran red.

By the time of the war, the great road from Baltimore to the West had already pushed far beyond the valleys through which the violent national conflict raged. (The *inter*national conflict, as those with Southern sympathies will insist.) The railroad too, had reached and passed its original destination.

There had been, however, a third attempt to reach the west: the Chesapeake and Ohio Canal. Originating in Georgetown rather than in Baltimore, it snaked westward along the twisting course of the Potomac River. Although it was begun in 1828, the same year that saw ground broken for the B & O Railroad, the canal's builders were plagued by problems and delays. Consequently, the C & O did not reach Cumberland until 1850. Technologically obsolete by then, it was destined to go no further. With its narrow liftlocks (74 of them), its mule-power pace, and its bottle-neck tunnel at Paw Paw, the C & O was no match for the iron and steam of the railroad.

Today, many sections of the old waterway are very successfully playing new roles, roles that could never have been foreseen by the canal's original investors. Its towpath has become a bikeway and hiking trail. The stretches that have been restored and rewatered are popular picnic destinations.

A favorite is the length that skirts the Great Falls of the Potomac in Montgomery County. The Falls mark with considerable turbulence the spot where the Potomac rushes from its high Piedmont course down to its tidewater level through a dramatic series of cataracts and rapids. Here too, beside one of the rewatered locks, is the Great Falls Tavern, now a museum.

As the canal continues to companion the Potomac westward, it comes close to Fort Frederick. Partially restored, the fort was built in 1756 to defend what then was the colony's frontier against the French and Indians. From the height commanded by its thick stone bastions, the views of the Potomac valley are lovely indeed.

At Cumberland, the C & O ends, as we have observed. And at Cumberland, US 40, the old National Road, starts to swing gradually to the north. And, at Cumberland, the Potomac itself veers abruptly to the southwest. The wedge of land defined by these two now-diverging routes — the river and road — is Garrett County.

The westernmost of Maryland's counties, Garrett is, despite strip-mining operations, largely a region of unspoiled natural beauty — a region of 3,000-foot mountains, of wild rivers rushing through dense forests, of scenic Muddy Creek and Swallow Falls, and of Deep Creek Lake, the largest lake in Maryland. (Like all the state's lakes, Deep Creek is man-made.) Summer in Garrett brings canoeing and kayaking, camping and fishing and trailblazing. Winter, as one would expect, brings some very good skiing.

Actually, any season in any part of Maryland brings its own special delight.

That, of course is hardly a new or an original observation. Back in 1608, when he was exploring what was to become Maryland, Captain John Smith himself called the place he saw a "delightsome land."

It was then.

It is now.